AMAZING TECHNOLOGY JOBS

COLIN HYNSON

Published in paperback in Great Britain
in 2019 by Wayland
Copyright © Hodder and Stoughton, 2016
All rights reserved

Editor: Victoria Brooker
Produced by Tall Tree Ltd
Editor: Jon Richards
Designer: Darren Jordan

ISBN: 978 1 5263 0007 2
10 9 8 7 6 5 4 3 2 1

Wayland
An imprint of Hachette
Children's Group
Part of Hodder and Stoughton
Carmelite House
50 Victoria Embankment
London EC4Y 0DZ

An Hachette UK Company
www.hachette.co.uk
www.hachettechildrens.co.uk

Printed and bound in China

MIX
Paper from
responsible sources
FSC® C104740

Picture credits

2 Dreamstime.com/Eugensergeev; 3 Dreamstime.com/Eduard Bonnin Turina; 4 Dreamstime.com/Kts; 5t NASA, 5c Dreamstime.com/Maislam; 6b Dreamstime.com/Mimagephotography, 6–7 Dreamstime.com/Wavebreakmedia Ltd; 8–9 Dreamstime.com/Georgil Dolgykh, 9 Dreamstime.com/Mast3r; 10b Anna Frodesiak, 10–11 Dreamstime.com/Jesse Lee Lang, 12 Dreamstime.com/Dacstyle, 12–13 Dreamstime.com/Mast3r; 14b Dreamstime.com/sasalan999, 14–15 Dreamstime.com/Martinmark; 16b Dreamstime.com/Urii Stepanov, 16–17 Dreamstime.com/Dmitriy Shironosov; 18t Dreamstime.com/Igor Akimov, 18–19 Dreamstime.com/Eduard Bonnin Turina; 20 Dreamstime.com/Belahoche, 21c Dreamstime.com/Sigur1, 21t Jeremykemp; 23c Dreamstime.com/Eugensergeev, 23b Dreamstime.com/Vladgalenko; 24–25 Dreamstime.com/Dikliy; 26b NASA, 26–27 NASA, 27t NASA; 28–29 Dreamstime.com/Donvictorio; 31 Dreamstime.com/Georgil Dolgykh.

CONTENTS

TECHNOLOGY

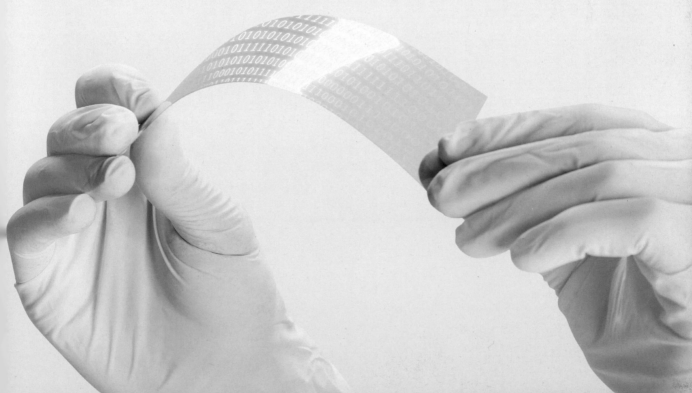

JOBS IN TECHNOLOGY

A QUALIFICATION IN TECHNOLOGY WILL EQUIP YOU TO CREATE EVERYTHING FROM MOVIE SPECIAL EFFECTS TO SPACE PROBES

Welcome to the world of working in technology. Studying technology is really worthwhile, because it opens doors to a whole range of interesting, exciting and unusual jobs — amazing jobs in technology.

Studying technology doesn't mean you'll be stuck in a laboratory or staring at a computer screen. There are jobs in artificial intelligence, nanotechnology and video games. Find out what each job is all about, as well as the rewards of doing the job.

▶ Nanorobots may be able to use microtechnology to cure diseases that are currently untreatable by conventional medicine.

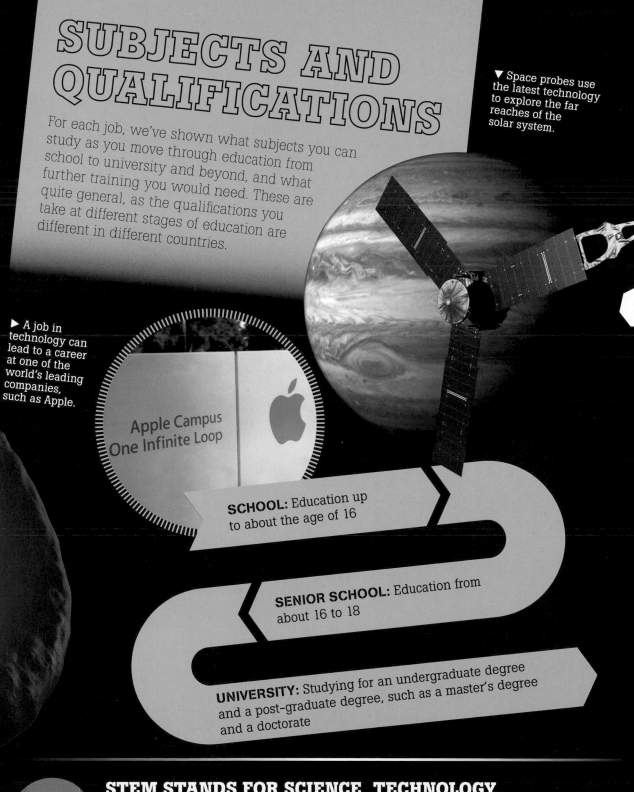

SUBJECTS AND QUALIFICATIONS

For each job, we've shown what subjects you can study as you move through education from school to university and beyond, and what further training you would need. These are quite general, as the qualifications you take at different stages of education are different in different countries.

▼ Space probes use the latest technology to explore the far reaches of the solar system.

▶ A job in technology can lead to a career at one of the world's leading companies, such as Apple.

Apple Campus
One Infinite Loop

SCHOOL: Education up to about the age of 16

SENIOR SCHOOL: Education from about 16 to 18

UNIVERSITY: Studying for an undergraduate degree and a post-graduate degree, such as a master's degree and a doctorate

STEM STANDS FOR SCIENCE, TECHNOLOGY, ENGINEERING AND MATHS. AS SCIENCE, TECHNOLOGY, AND ENGINEERING INDUSTRIES GROW, THERE IS INCREASING DEMAND FOR PEOPLE WITH STEM SKILLS.

BUILDING A CLOUD

CLOUD ARCHITECTS ARE HELPING TO SHAPE THE DIGITAL WORLD.

Cloud computing is one of the fastest growing parts of the world of information technology (IT) and offers lots of exciting opportunities for anybody who wants a job in computing. Cloud computing lets you store data or run software over the internet rather than on a hard drive. This means that you can access information wherever you are.

▼ With data stored on the cloud, your computer hard drive can be smaller, making your computer lighter and more portable.

▼ Using the cloud allows you to store thousands of digital photos and access them from any digital device.

WHAT YOU DO

The working day of a cloud architect will be varied. Even though much of your time will be spent designing and creating the cloud platform needed, you will also be part of a team looking after the computing needs of the organisation you are working for. There will be opportunities to work at different places. If you are working for a large organisation, there will be plenty of chances to work at different locations and with lots of different people.

THERE ARE THREE TYPES OF CLOUD. THERE IS THE PUBLIC CLOUD, WHICH ANYONE CAN ACCESS, THE PRIVATE CLOUD, WHICH ONLY CERTAIN PEOPLE CAN ACCESS, AND THE HYBRID CLOUD, WHICH IS A COMBINATION OF THE TWO.

WHERE YOU WORK

Just about every large organisation and business is either using cloud computing or is moving over to it. This means that you can combine your expertise in computing with any other interest or passion you might have. If you are interested in music, sport or films, you can work in cloud computing and be part of that industry.

SCHOOL: Maths, science and computing

THE ROUTE TO

SENIOR SCHOOL: Maths, science and computing

CLOUD COMPUTING

UNIVERSITY: It's best to study computer science. Some universities do offer advanced degrees (called master's degrees) in cloud computing.

BY THE END OF 2016, ABOUT 36 PER CENT OF ALL DATA WILL BE STORED IN THE CLOUD, UP FROM 7 PER CENT IN 2013.

DEVELOPING APPS

THE GROWTH IN MOBILE TECH IS GOOD FOR ANYONE WHO WANTS TO DEVELOP APPS.

As an app developer you would create the code that runs an app. You might also be involved in designing the look of the app as well as researching how people will want to use it.

Once the app has been created, you may be involved in testing it to make sure that it works properly. Even after the app has been released, you will still have to keep working on it. The world of app development is a fast-moving one and you will need to keep your app up-to-date.

WHAT YOU DO

Your working day will change as your app develops. While you are creating the app you will be spending a lot of time at your desk writing the code needed for the app. When the app is being tested and is then released to the public, you may find yourself moving between working at your desk and working with others as part of a team.

▲ Apps allow smartphones and tablets to carry out a wide range of tasks, from showing you recipes and cooking techniques to ordering taxis and plotting routes.

EMPLOYERS MAY ASK IF YOU HAVE MADE ANY APPS BEFORE. THIS WILL SHOW THEM THAT YOU HAVE SOME UNDERSTANDING ABOUT HOW APPS WORK AND HOW TO MAKE THEM. YOU CAN PROBABLY START MAKING YOUR OWN SIMPLE APPS AT SENIOR SCHOOL OR UNIVERSITY.

THE ROUTE TO
APP DEVELOPMENT

SCHOOL: Maths, science and computing

SENIOR SCHOOL: Maths, science (especially physics), computing and art and design

UNIVERSITY: Computer science is best. There are some universities that offer classes in app development as part of a degree in computer science.

▶ As an app developer you're likely to be part of a team, but there are many apps that are created by a single person.

THE LATEST ESTIMATE IS THAT THERE ARE ABOUT 3 MILLION APPS AVAILABLE – BUT THAT NUMBER IS GROWING BY 2,000 EVERY DAY.

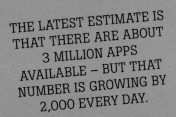

WHERE YOU WORK

Many of the businesses and organisations that use apps do not produce the apps themselves. They usually work with a company that specialises in creating apps. If you work for one of these companies, you'll find that the kind of work you're involved in is really varied. You might be working at your local zoo one day and then you'll be at a major film studio working on an app for their next blockbuster movie the next day.

INFERNO ARTIST

A VISUAL EFFECTS ARTIST CREATES FILM SCENES THAT WOULD BE TOO DANGEROUS, TOO EXPENSIVE OR JUST IMPOSSIBLE TO FILM.

As a Visual Effects Artist (also known as an Inferno Artist) you will create movie special effects using computer generated imagery (CGI). Visual Effects Artists need to have both technological and artistic skills. Every film is planned using a storyboard. Once this has been agreed, you will be able to see where the visual effects are needed. Visual Effects Artists are not normally involved with the actual filming. Your work really begins when filming ends, a stage that's called post–production.

▲ A storyboard is a series of drawings that show the story behind the film being made.

WHAT YOU DO

There are lots of different people who are involved with the post–production part of a film or television programme. This means that your typical working day will be a mixture of being in front of a computer creating the visual effects you have been asked to create as well as working with everybody else involved in post–production. Visual Effects Artists are sometimes asked to work long hours to fit in with the schedule for the film or television programme.

IF YOU ARE WORKING WITH A BIG POST-PRODUCTION COMPANY THEN YOU CAN HAVE THE CHANCE TO SPECIALISE IN A PARTICULAR AREA OF SPECIAL EFFECTS, SUCH AS CREATING FANTASTIC LANDSCAPES.

WHERE YOU WORK

Although you might expect to work for a film or television company, most Visual Effects Artists work for companies that specialise in providing post–production expertise. If you work for one of these companies, you'll be involved in all sorts of different projects where visual effects are needed. One day you'll be creating special effects for a major movie and the next day the visual effects for a new car advert.

▼ This mountain scene was created using CGI and may be placed behind actors in post–production so that they can film in a studio rather than on location, which may be more expensive.

SCHOOL: Maths, Science, computer science, art

THE ROUTE TO

SENIOR SCHOOL: Science (especially physics), maths, computer science and art and design

VISUAL EFFECTS ARTIST

UNIVERSITY: There are some universities that offer degrees in computer animation and visual effects. However, a degree in computer science is also useful.

DIGITAL PROTECTION

FIGHT CRIME WITH SOME SERIOUS TECH SKILLS AND QUALIFICATIONS.

12 Cybercrime takes lots of different forms and affects everyone from large businesses to individual people. If you want to be in the front line of the defence against cybercrime then you can work in cyber-security. Your main job will be to try and protect computer information by using tools like firewalls (which block malware from getting into a computer) or creating encryption codes.

```
Aircrack PTW cont

        Aircrack-

[00:02:05] Tested 11238 keys

byte(vote)
77(24320)  D9(24320)  7E(24064)
91(24064)  4E(23808)  AB(23808)
39(27392)  8B(26368)  BD(26368)
38(26112)  8C(25600)  87(24832)
30(26880)  4D(26880)  FC(25856)

    KEY FOUND! [ 77:34:39:38:
ed correctly: 100%
```

◀ Part of your time will be trying to crack your own encryption to try and find any weaknesses.

WHAT YOU DO

The methods used by cyber criminals are constantly changing, so part of your job will involve keeping up with changing methods of cybercrime. There are new malware threats appearing all the time and they are getting better at breaking through firewalls and hiding themselves on a computer network so that people don't know they are there. You'll have to improve the security levels on your computer network to fight off these new threats.

GOVERNMENTS ARE OFFERING IMAGINATIVE WAYS TO GET YOUNG PEOPLE INTERESTED. FOR EXAMPLE, THE DEPARTMENT FOR HOMELAND SECURITY IN THE US HOLDS CYBER-SECURITY CAMPS AND STUDY DAYS.

THE ROUTE

SCHOOL: Maths, science and computer science

SENIOR SCHOOL: Science, maths and computer science

TO CYBER-SECURITY

UNIVERSITY: Computer science or maths

WHERE YOU WORK

As cyber-security becomes more important, the number of businesses that specialise in protecting computer networks is growing. They can protect the computer networks of large and small organisations. People in cyber-security can also work for the armed forces, the police or for security services.

▶ Much of your time will be spent analysing attempted attacks by cyber criminals.

IN ONE SINGLE SECURITY BREACH IN 2011, THE PERSONAL DETAILS OF MORE THAN 77 MILLION PEOPLE WERE STOLEN BY HACKERS FROM SONY'S VIDEO GAME ONLINE NETWORK.

THE INTERNET OF THINGS

HELP TO CREATE A WORLD WHERE OBJECTS AND MACHINES TALK TO EACH OTHER.

Imagine a world where there are 'smart' objects with computer chips that collect and share information across the internet. This is called the Internet of Things. As the Internet of Things grows there will be more and more demand for people who can work in a wide range of disciplines. The collection of enormous amounts of data will lead to career opportunities in cloud computing, cyber-security and data analysis.

◀ Bridges can be fitted with sensors that detect traffic levels and monitor for signs of wear and tear.

THE ROUTE TO

SCHOOL: Maths, science and computer science

SENIOR SCHOOL: Science, maths and computer science

THE INTERNET OF THINGS

UNIVERSITY: Computer science. Some universities offer classes on the Internet of Things as part of a degree in computing.

THERE ARE TECHNOLOGY COMPANIES THAT ARE DEVELOPING WAYS OF USING THE INTERNET OF THINGS TO HELP US LOOK AFTER OURS PETS. 'SMART' BOWLS WILL TELL US WHEN OUR CAT OR DOG NEEDS SOME FRESH FOOD.

WHERE YOU WORK

Because the Internet of Things can be applied to almost any industry, there are few limitations as to who you could end up working with. It could be a large construction company or a firm making the latest wearable technology. Every day, new potential career opportunities are opening up in this exciting world.

◀ Smartwatches can record your exercise routines, monitor your physical health and send information to your doctor.

WHAT YOU DO

Working in the Internet of Things means a lot of variety in your working day. There are many people working in this industry and you will have to cooperate with all of them during your working day. You will be working with the designers and manufacturers of 'smart' objects as well as with people who work on the computing side.

DESIGN THE EXPERIENCE

FIND OUT HOW TECHNOLOGY CAN IMPROVE THE WAY PEOPLE USE THINGS.

Every product that we use has been designed. In the digital world, the User Experience (UX) Designer makes sure that a website, app or computer game has the right 'feel' to it. The UX Designer is concerned with the 'findability' and the 'usability' of the app. Findability is how easy it is for somebody to find what they are looking for in the app. Usability is about how people will navigate around the app and whether they need any complicated instructions before they start.

YOU WILL CREATE SOMETHING CALLED A PERSONA OR A USER MODEL – A FICTIONAL CHARACTER THAT WILL HELP WITH THE DESIGN OF THE NEW PRODUCT.

▶ Any app you design must be easy to find and easy to use.

WHAT YOU DO

Your working day as a UX Designer will be a varied one. Some of your time will be spent in front of a computer creating Personas and Wireframes for a new product. However, you will also have to be away from your desk quite a lot. UX Designers have to organise groups of people to test any prototypes in lots of different locations.

WHERE YOU WORK

Just about every technology company making digital products, such as websites, apps or games will need the expertise of a UX Designer. Larger companies will employ their own UX Designers. There are also specialist companies that supply UX Design services to smaller businesses. Many businesses also make sure that the UX Designer is the same person who actually designs the product.

▶ Part of your role will be testing any product with members of the public to see how they use and react to it.

THE ROUTE TO UX DESIGN

SCHOOL: Computer science, maths, science and art

SENIOR SCHOOL: Science, maths, computer science and art and design

UNIVERSITY: Computer science, computer–aided design. There are some universities that offer advanced classes in UX Design.

THE ACTUAL DESIGN OF A DIGITAL PRODUCT IS DONE BY A USER INTERFACE (UI) DESIGNER. IF YOU DO BOTH OF THESE JOBS THEN YOU COULD BE CALLED A VISUAL DESIGNER.

TINY TECH

DESIGN AND BUILD OBJECTS AND MACHINES THAT ARE FAR TOO SMALL TO SEE.

18

▼ This nanotechnology laboratory in Russia uses highly specialist equipment to create devices and materials.

Engineers and scientists who work in the field of nanotechnology are creating devices and materials on a very small scale. You'll be working with materials between 1 and 10 nanometres in size. To give you an idea of how small that is, the thickness of a sheet of paper in this book is about 100,000 nanometres.

Nanotechnlogy is being used in a wide range of industries, including computing, energy production and medicine. Nanotechnologists can produce lighter and stronger materials and electronic devices that are smaller, faster and more portable.

WHERE YOU WORK

Because nanotechnology is spreading into so many technology sectors you'll find that there are plenty of opportunities to work in this area. You may find yourself working for businesses that specialise in electronics, energy production and storage, transport, materials science, medicine or food production.

If you are working as a nanotechnologist then a lot of your time will be spent creating and testing new devices and materials. These materials are usually made in 'clean rooms'. This means that the area you are working in will be as free as possible from any kind of contaminate, especially dust. Any new devices and materials will still have to be tested outside of the laboratory to make sure that they work in the real world. You may be involved in this testing as well.

THE ROUTE TO NANOTECHNOLOGY

SCHOOL: Computer science, maths and science

SENIOR SCHOOL: Science (especially physics), maths and computer science

UNIVERSITY: Computer science, physics, maths, chemistry, materials science. Some universities offer advanced courses in nanotechnology.

▲ This flexible transparent screen was created using nanotechnology materials. It could be used to display video calls or movies before being rolled up and put away.

NANOROBOTS ARE TINY DEVICES THAT CAN BE INJECTED INTO A PATIENT AND USED TO HELP REPAIR DAMAGED CELLS OR TO SEEK OUT AND DESTROY VIRUSES OR CANCER CELLS.

THINKING MACHINES

TECHNOLOGY SKILLS CAN HELP TO BUILD MACHINES THAT WILL THINK AND DO FOR THEMSELVES.

▼ Artificial intelligence may also be used to create 'smart' artificial limbs.

The rise of artificial intelligence (AI), or machine learning, makes it possible for machines to make decisions themselves. They do not need people to give instructions. We can already see examples of AI today. Driverless cars are being tested on our roads and internet search engines use it to help trawl the web. AI can also be found in video games and even in some hospitals.

THE ROUTE TO ARTIFICIAL INTELLIGENCE

SCHOOL: Computer science, maths and science

SENIOR SCHOOL: Science, maths and computer science

UNIVERSITY: Computer science. Some universities offer courses on artificial intelligence as part of their computer science degree.

AUTOMATIC ROAD TRANSPORT SYSTEM

robosoft

RESEARCH IS BEING DONE INTO CREATING A 'VIRTUAL COMPANION' FOR ELDERLY PEOPLE. IT CAN MONITOR THE HEALTH OF THE PERSON IT IS LOOKING AFTER AND CAN CONTACT MEDICAL SERVICES IF NEEDED.

WHERE YOU WORK

Nearly every technology company is currently looking into how they can use artificial intelligence in their products. If you want to work in artificial intelligence then you can combine it with another interest, such as medicine, games design or robotics.

▼ This driverless minibus is being tested on the streets of León, Spain.

▲ This robot at a hospital in the US is delivering medicines to where they are needed.

CITY DEMONSTRATIONS

CityMobil2

WHAT YOU DO

If you are working in artificial intelligence then you will be spending much of your day developing and testing intelligent machines. This may mean using a computer to write the programming language needed for the machine to operate properly. You will also be involved in the design and creation of the machines themselves, so you will be working with designers and engineers.

DRONE PILOT

THIS TECHNOLOGY CAN TAKE YOU TO THE OTHER SIDE OF THE WORLD, WITHOUT YOU LEAVING YOUR OFFICE.

Drones (or Unmanned Aerial Vehicles – UAVs) are planes that fly without a pilot on board. Drones are used by the military, but are moving into other areas of life, including law enforcement agencies, journalism and deliveries. Like many technology jobs, working with drones will allow you to combine your love of all things technological with the chance to work in lots of different areas. The drones of the future will have to be designed and built, while the software used to control them will also have to be written and continually updated.

▲ This military drone is used to deliver medical supplies to remote bases.

WHAT YOU DO

If you are working with drones, then some of your time will be in the laboratory or factory as part of the team designing and building the aircraft. Different jobs will need different kinds of drone so you'll be involved in lots of new projects. Once the drone has been built, you will have to spend some time testing it outside to check that it's working properly.

THE ROUTE TO A CAREER WITH

SCHOOL: Computer science, maths and science

SENIOR SCHOOL: Science (especially physics), maths, computer science and design

UNIVERSITY: Computer science and engineering. There are also drone training colleges that can teach you how to design, build and control drones.

DRONES

▼ Drones can either be flown by a person on the ground or by using its own computer program.

WHERE YOU WORK

There are lots of technology companies that are exploring how they may be able to use drones in their work. At the moment, drones are mostly used by the police and armed forces. However, in the future you may find yourself working for delivery companies, TV and film companies or with organisations helping people in disaster-hit regions.

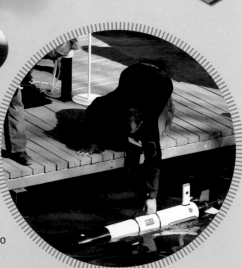

▶ A submersible drone is lowered into the waters of a lake.

SOME DRONES DON'T FLY — THEY SWIM! SUBMERSIBLE DRONES HAVE BEEN USED TO SEARCH FOR THE WRECKAGE OF AIRCRAFT THAT HAVE CRASHED FAR OUT AT SEA.

GAMES DEVELOPER

BE PART OF A TECH INDUSTRY THAT'S USED BY MILLIONS OF PEOPLE EVERY SINGLE DAY.

If you are thinking about becoming a games developer, you will have to decide on an area that you would like to specialise in. Today's computer games are usually so complex that they require a large team of people working together. You may decide to become a game programmer, creating the code that actually makes the game run. Game designers create the look of the game, developing characters, settings, how the game plays and the different levels.

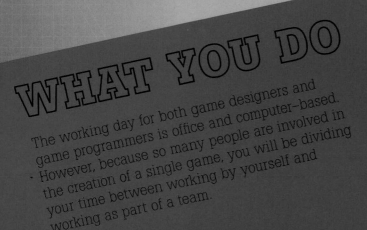

WHAT YOU DO

The working day for both game designers and game programmers is office and computer-based. However, because so many people are involved in the creation of a single game, you will be dividing your time between working by yourself and working as part of a team.

THE ROUTE

SCHOOL: Computer science, maths and science

SENIOR SCHOOL: Science (especially physics), maths, computer science and design

TO GAMES DEVELOPMENT

UNIVERSITY: Computer games design, computer science, graphic design

WHERE YOU WORK

There are a large number of companies who create computer games. All of them are looking for games developers to meet growing demand for new games. There are plenty of opportunities to work abroad as many of these companies have offices in different countries.

◀ Games developers need to create an immersive experience, complete with realistic graphics and sounds.

THE GLOBAL VIDEO GAMES MARKET IS EXPECTED TO BE WORTH NEARLY US$119 BILLION A YEAR BY 2019.

INTO SPACE

THIS JOB WILL TAKE YOU FAR BEYOND EARTH AND OUT INTO SPACE.

On 19 January 2006, a space probe called *New Horizons* launched from Cape Canaveral. Eight years later it arrived at the dwarf planet Pluto. On board were instruments to study the atmosphere and the surface of Pluto as well as cameras to take pictures. *New Horizons* is now travelling to the outer reaches of our solar system. Today, most space exploration is carried out by probes, because it is impossible to send people on very long journeys.

▼ The NASA team celebrates when it receives confirmation that *New Horizons* (right) has reached Pluto.

WHAT YOU DO

If you are involved in a space probe project, your role will change over time. When the space probe is being designed and built, you will be part of a team working both in a laboratory and at Mission Control (the place where the flight of the space probe is managed). However, it may take several years for the space probe to reach its destination. During that time, you may work on other projects. Once the probe is near its place of arrival then you will be back in Mission Control to start communicating with the space probe.

SOME SPACE AGENCIES RUN SUMMER CAMPS FOR YOUNG PEOPLE WHERE YOU COULD GET THE CHANCE TO COMMUNICATE WITH A SPACE PROBE AND COME UP WITH IDEAS FOR FUTURE SPACE EXPERIMENTS.

WHERE YOU WORK

If you want to work in the development of space probes, you will probably be working for a government space programme. This could be NASA in the United States or the European Space Agency. China, Japan and India also have their own space agencies.

▶ Space probes don't just orbit or fly past planets. Some are rovers that explore the surface of another planet. The *Curiosity* rover is studying the geology of Mars.

THE ROUTE TO
SPACE PROBE
DEVELOPMENT

SCHOOL: Computer science, maths and science

SENIOR SCHOOL: Science (especially physics), maths and computer science

UNIVERSITY: Computer science, physics and planetary science

ETHICAL HACKING

USE YOUR TECH SKILLS TO BREAK INTO OTHER PEOPLES' COMPUTERS – LEGALLY!

To protect themselves from hacking attacks, some organisations actually organise an attack on their own computer network to find any weaknesses first.
If you are interested in a career in cyber-security then you might want to become a penetration tester (also called an ethical hacker). You will be asked to organise a hacking attack on a computer network.

▼ Many government security organisations, such as the FBI in Washington, DC (below), employ hackers to test their own systems.

WHAT YOU DO

As an ethical hacker much of your working day will be spent communicating with the people inside the organisation whose computer network you are trying to break into. They have to know what you are doing and when you are planning to do it. You will have to spend quite a lot of time planning your hacking activities before you actually start. You will also need to keep up-to-date with the latest techniques and technologies used by cyber criminals.

IF YOU WANT TO WORK AS AN ETHICAL HACKER THEN YOU HAVE TO CONVINCE WHOEVER IS USING YOU THAT YOU CAN BE TRUSTED. AFTER ALL, YOU ARE TRYING TO BREAK INTO THEIR COMPUTER NETWORK.

IN 2001–2002, GARY MCKINNON FROM THE UK HACKED INTO 97 COMPUTERS AT THE US NAVY, ARMY, PENTAGON AND NASA. HE CLAIMED HE WAS LOOKING FOR GOVERNMENT FILES ABOUT ALIENS.

WHERE YOU WORK

There are a few companies that specialise in offering ethical hacking to businesses. However, you will probably work for a company that offers more general cyber-security support. Some of the larger technology companies may employ their own cyber-security staff and this could include people skilled in hacking.

THE ROUTE TO ETHICAL HACKING

SCHOOL: Computer science, maths and science

SENIOR SCHOOL: Science (especially physics), maths and computer science

UNIVERSITY: Computer science

GLOSSARY

APP
Software that is designed to run on smartphones and tablets.

ARTIFICIAL INTELLIGENCE
Computers that can independently perform tasks that usually require human intelligence.

CLOUD COMPUTING
Storing and accessing computing data through the internet rather than from a hard drive.

CODE
A set of instructions made up of letters and numbers that is read by computer software.

CYBERCRIME
Criminal activities carried out using computers and the internet.

CYBER-SECURITY
The technology and practices needed to protect computers from attacks from cyber criminals.

DRONE
A vehicle that can be navigated either automatically or from a distance.

ENCRYPTION
The conversion of computer data so that it can only be read by selected people.

FINDABILITY
The ease with which somebody can find what they want on a piece of software.

FIREWALL
A computer security system that controls what is going out of or coming into a computer system.

GRAPHICS
The design of images that are used on websites, apps or advertising.

HACKING
Gaining unauthorised access to a computer system.

HARD DRIVE
The hard drive controls the use of a hard disc inside a computer.

INFORMATION TECHNOLOGY
The technology involved in the use and maintenance of computer systems, including both the hardware and software.

MALWARE
Software designed to disrupt or destroy computer systems.

MASTER'S DEGREE
A university degree that is a higher level than a first, or bachelor's, degree.

MISSION CONTROL
The command centre for controlling and supporting space flights.

NANOMETRE
A very small unit of measurement. A single nanometre measures just one billionth of a metre.

NANOROBOT
A tiny machine with parts that can be measured in nanometres.

NANOTECHNOLOGY
The use of technology and engineering at a nanoscale. Normally between one and 100 nanometres.

PERSONA
Personas are created by UX designers. They are fictional characters based on the kind of person who will use a new product.

POST-PRODUCTION
Work done on a film after the filming has been completed.

SMART OBJECTS
Everyday objects like fridges that have a computer chip which collects and shares information across the internet.

SMARTWATCHES
A tiny computer worn on the wrist. It can be used for lots of things, such as monitoring the health of the wearer.

STORYBOARD
A series of drawings created before a film is made. The storyboard shows the story behind a movie.

SUBMERSIBLE
A drone that operates underwater.

UNDERGRADUATE
A person who is studying at a university for their first degree.

USABILITY
This is the measurement of how simple it is to use an app or a piece of software.

VISUAL EFFECTS
The creation of images in a film that cannot be created in a live-action shot.

WIREFRAME
A rough layout of a product that is being developed.

INDEX